We hope you enjoy this book. Please return or renew it by the due date.

NML esp

You can renew it at www.norfolk.gov.uk/libraries or by using our free library app.

Otherwise you can phone 0344 800 8020 - please have your library card and PIN ready.

You can sign up for email reminders too.

24/03/22

D1342213

NORFOLK ITEM

30129 085 771 112

UNCONSCIOUS BIAS

An Hachette UK Company
www.hachette.co.uk

Summersdale Publishers Ltd
Part of Octopus Publishing Group Limited
Carmelite House
50 Victoria Embankment
LONDON
EC4Y 0DZ
UK

www.summersdale.com

Printed and bound in Malta

ISBN: 978-1-78783-973-1

Substantial discounts on bulk quantities of Summersdale books are available to corporations, professional associations and other organizations. For details contact general enquiries: telephone: +44 (0) 1243 771107 or email: enquiries@summersdale.com.

UNCONSCIOUS
BIAS

Everything You Need to Know About Our Hidden Prejudices

ANNIE BURDICK

summersdale

CONTENTS

Introduction

We live in a connected world and interact with many people, whether directly or in passing, most days of our lives. What makes these interactions interesting and meaningful is not our similarities, but that we are unique individuals living wonderfully varied lives.

Our diversity offers us so much. It gives us the opportunity to learn from each other and develop our own communities within the world. It lets us build skills, knowledge and understanding. When we open ourselves up to connecting with a wide and diverse group of people, there is so much more that we're able to learn.

So why do we have bias? It is a part of human life, just as diversity is, yet it is an aspect of our nature that draws us apart. Bias is woven into the fabric of our interactions and conversations, just as much as it is instilled deep in our brains and reactions.

We can't always see it. Sometimes we choose not to. Nonetheless, it is there, altering and affecting the interactions that people have with each other, around the world, every day.

Bias comes in many forms. It takes on other names and transforms into similar negative manifestations, such as prejudice, discrimination and injustice. This book will start by providing a basic introduction to these concepts and the way that bias appears in our world. The second chapter expands on this and provides some real-world examples of how bias appears. Finally, the third chapter aims to offer actionable guidance and support to help you conquer biases of your own.

Even as we become more connected as a planet, negativity and discrimination are not fading away, as it seems they should. And they won't go away on their own. Each of us as individuals has the power to acknowledge our bias, rather than ignore it. We each have the power to learn about the impact of bias in our world. We have the power to undo our unconscious biases actively and live our lives with empathy and acceptance.

This book is here to teach you why these powers are important and how to claim them.

Chapter One

WHAT IS UNCONSCIOUS BIAS?

Bias is part of our world, as prevalent as diversity and originality. There are billions of us, a collection of many races, sexualities, nationalities, genders and religions, encompassing a vast range of ages, sizes and abilities. This is a wonderful thing. Our differences make us human and they make us interesting. Our differences and our diversity mean that each of us has something unique to offer to the world and to the conversation. When we can see that in each other, bias starts to fall away.

But until then, bias does exist, all around us, every day. There is bias in each of us.

Most of the time we experience bias unconsciously. However, that doesn't mean that we don't act on our unconscious biases. Or that we shouldn't work to undo them. The goal of this book is to acknowledge and understand that, then turn it on its head, demonstrating how to be actively unbiased – at least as far as is possible – instead. The first step is understanding what bias is and how it is created. That's where we'll start.

Let's invite one another in.
Maybe then we can begin
to fear less, to make fewer
wrong assumptions, to let go
of the biases and stereotypes
that unnecessarily divide us.

MICHELLE OBAMA

BIAS CAN BE COMPLICATED, BUT LOVE IS THE SIMPLEST STARTING POINT

Bias: The Basics

Bias, both conscious and unconscious, is a complex concept. And whether in subtle or noticeable ways it influences all of us and the society we all take part in, every day. We'll start here with the most basic overview of bias and build up to understanding more of the concept and how to reframe it in our own lives.

In a general sense, bias is a tendency to see something – whether a person, group, experience or thing – through a certain lens or with a particular slant, either positive or negative. In essence, it's being in favour of or against something, even without specific evidence or reasoning behind the feeling, or without considering a different inclination.

Bias is often synonymous with prejudice, partiality, one-sidedness or non-objectivity, so these words, which you may often hear in the news, are often simply referring to a person's or group's bias.

This Is About All of Us

Everyone experiences or feels some degree of bias, even if it is unconscious or internal. You don't have to act on your bias to have it. You also may not realize that you *are* making decisions or actions based on unconscious biases. Biases are formed in many ways throughout our lives (which we'll discuss later on), so all of us have some, whether or not they're easy to recognize.

Often they can also be uncomfortable to recognize, and we may avoid acknowledging our own internal bias to escape the feeling that we're doing something wrong or that we're being racist, sexist, homophobic, ageist and so on. But the first step to becoming actively and consciously *unbiased* – the path this book aims to set you on – is to look at your own thoughts and reactions and recognize that you, like everyone else in the world, has unconscious bias.

This book is not here to target specific people. It's here to remind you that *every* person has some biases, whether or not they express them aloud. We can all do better for each other.

Conscious vs Unconscious

It's important to explore the differences between biases that are conscious and those that are unconscious. It's possible that you have some of both, though it's fair to hope that more people now are unconsciously biased as opposed to actively and consciously biased. Even if that's not the case, in order to emerge as a more consciously unbiased person, it's essential to understand the differences between the two and how to recognize them so that you're later able to move past them.

Conscious Bias

- Done intentionally and knowingly. An active choice to be biased against someone or something.
- We recognize we are being biased toward a person or group and choose to accept it.
- This is more blatant and can have consequences in the workplace or socially if exposed.
- Often results in a person making conscious discriminatory choices or actions.

Unconscious Bias

- Often done or felt without realizing.
- Typically based on our world views or experiences subliminally affecting our active thought processes.
- Often occurs during moments of decision-making or judgement.
- Each person's are unique.
- Can still lead to real-world discrimination, even without conscious recognition of the reasoning.

Why This Difference Is Important

The difference between conscious and unconscious bias is important. Becoming consciously unbiased takes acknowledgement and work. If you're starting with unconscious bias, the work comes from paying attention to your thoughts and judgements. By noting the biases you have but didn't previously recognize, you can actively begin to undo them. If you're beginning with conscious biases, you already know they're there. Moving away from these biases has a different starting point but can involve many of the same bias-beating techniques.

Unfortunately, unconscious bias is deeply rooted in our lives. It's a reaction to lived experience, and it's something that everyone has, even if only in small doses. Unconscious bias can negatively affect our perceptions of other people and it can impact our expectations or make us subconsciously avoid people or experiences. It can also lead to unintentional but real exclusion or cause pain. In order to move our society to a more accepting place, it is important for us all to move past unconscious bias.

Sources of Bias: The Basics

Unconscious bias develops naturally over the course of life experiences, social interactions and information our brains take in repeatedly over time. This is why it's nearly impossible to avoid developing some form of bias, however small. We all go out into the world and have experiences and interactions that shape how we will view other people, groups and situations in the future. Our brains automatically make generalizations, associations and categorizations, without any of it meaning we're being intentionally discriminatory or prejudiced. These are some of the many things that can cause bias:

- Brain shortcuts and "common sense" decisions (our brains are hardwired to make quick decisions when needed, based on the information we already have and the basic things we think are true or logical).

- Personal traumas and negative experiences.

- Cultural norms, expectations and stereotypes.

- Social media, news media and advertising.

- Influence of family members or friends.

- Childhood experiences.

- Bias of groups you belong to (whether a religion, ethnic group or social group you've joined).

We will look at these in more depth over the following pages.

The Evolution Connection

The effect of evolution on our psychology is a complex topic still being studied and explored by bright minds around the world. Many evolutionary psychologists believe there may be a link between our evolutionary drives to survive and reproduce and the more modern concept of unconscious bias. Essentially, to simplify a complicated concept, we have evolved to react to perceived threats and opportunities in whatever way will be most beneficial to us, to our individual survival. Our brains are still wired for survival and reducing errors in judgement, even when it may no longer seem that way.

So on a deep psychological level, bias may also have roots in this innate need to make the best and fastest choice based on the information available, all for the good of being able to go on living and reproducing. Though you may never consciously think this way, some deep internal part of you may be hardwired to do so. Bias is a result when these evolutionary, decision-making instincts meet the other many sources of bias you're exposed to.

Pattern Seeking

Much of the time bias is psychological, based on the brain's natural functions, and only partially influenced by outside stimuli. The brain is the most powerful force when it comes to unconscious bias. It stores all of the instincts, the messages, memories and common sense that make us think and act the way we do. Even when you think you don't harbour biases toward a person or group, your brain can disprove that.

As we go through life, the brain collects many millions of tiny pieces of information almost constantly and files them away, unconsciously categorizing and making patterns from the combination of new information and old information. This leads to a concept called pattern-seeking, the brain relying on things it's experienced and filed away in the past to make assumptions that future situations will follow the same patterns. For example, you may have had only female teachers during early education and are surprised to have a male teacher later on. In this scenario, your brain was pattern-seeking and therefore producing bias as a result.

Personal Experience

Amongst the most common sources of deep and unconscious bias are the experiences you have throughout your life. These are incredibly broad; they can include anything from discriminatory things you heard your relatives say while you were growing up to things other kids said in the classroom or a subject you studied in school.

Every person's life experiences are unique. Your brain develops its new thought processes and reactions based on past experiences. So it's no huge shock that a good or bad experience with someone from a particular demographic group can trigger a natural subconscious association that may persist for years, particularly if that association is enforced by additional experiences or other information your brain receives.

Bias also comes from the people you spend the most time with. Your parents, siblings, close friends and other loved ones have a great influence on the messages you hear and the biases you come into contact with. Everyone knows people in their lives who are openly biased. Think back to the time you spent with them when you were young and learning about the world. How much did their perspectives affect yours?

Society and Culture

Society surrounds us every day and has an effect on the messages our brains receive and interpret, whether or not we're actively engaging with them. Think of this first: do any parts of our global society make you feel negatively about an aspect of yourself? Perhaps you see messages in the way people treat beauty, weight, age, sexuality, wealth or relationship status, and they make you feel bad about the way you look, how you live your life, or any number of other things. This is society subtly enacting its bias upon your perceptions of yourself!

Now think of the ways those societal and cultural messages may affect how you feel bias toward others. Perhaps you see someone in a particular profession and find yourself surprised that someone of their gender, age, sexuality or race would have that job. Maybe you think critically of someone who looks "unhealthy" without knowing anything about their situation. You may make assumptions about someone who is very wealthy or poor, based on what our society has to say about these statuses. So often these biases and many others have roots and connections to our cultural expectations.

Traumatic and Painful Experiences

Just as you can learn unconscious bias from the more mundane and standard experiences of your life, the same can also apply to traumatic situations you may live through. Trauma has a deep psychological effect on a person and can cause strong and painful reactions, even years later, particularly from triggers.

Let's say, for example, that you had a traumatic experience perpetuated by someone of a particular race, gender or age. Your brain may have become unconsciously trained to fear or mistrust someone else of that background. Perhaps they look or sound alike, or live in a similar area. You're not actively or intentionally associating this group as being bad, but your brain still connects them with the trauma and thus associates them with a level of fear or other negative emotion.

This type of bias can be much harder to break or reshape, as the basis is such a deeply rooted and psychologically binding moment. The key here, as with any bias, is starting with recognition, and moving forward from there.

Social Media and Advertising

These forms of media have grown over the years to be among the most prevalent sources of bias. Being continuously bombarded with information and messages from friends, strangers, corporations, news media, advertisers and influencers takes a toll on our brains. It affects how we see each other.

Some of it is intentional. When a company wants to sell a product, they target certain demographics. This shows the company's bias, as well as biases they want to instil in their customers. When they hire models and influencers that look a certain way or are, for example, white, able-bodied or heterosexual, consumers note this, both consciously and subconsciously.

As we consume content on social media and elsewhere online, the things we see repeatedly reinforce stereotypes, judgements and biases. This happens with and without us knowing. When we recognize what we're being sold and fed by social media and advertisements, we're able to start moving toward actively undoing the biases we hold.

Stereotype Threat

Strange as it may sound, you can have biases against groups that you belong to. One version of this, most often arising in the education system, is called *stereotype threat*. This often comes into play in early schooling or during childhood, and it can continue to affect people later in college or in their young adulthood.

Essentially, stereotype threat refers to an issue in which people find themselves at risk of aligning with harmful biases about their social group, most often their race or gender, though not exclusively. It was first noted and studied in testing situations in 1995 with young students, who, when reminded of harmful stereotypes about their race or gender, performed worse on tests, because the biases were planted more firmly in their heads and affected their self-perceptions. They started to believe the negative statements made about them and their social groups – for instance, that Black students don't do as well on tests or that female students couldn't excel at maths or sciences. However, when the biases weren't emphasized or pointed out to them, they did just as well as the other students. Bias is powerful, even to ourselves.

Group Bias

Social groups have been biased toward one another for many thousands of years. One of the more typical examples is religion. For as long as religions have existed, they have held biases toward other religions or the non-religious, considering them lesser for not believing the same teachings or in the same god or gods. This is a mindset that often persists to this day. While many people of all faiths choose to respect and support others, there are others who are consciously or unconsciously swayed by the bias of their religious organization or specific church.

This concept goes for other groups as well. Particular ethnic groups or races are sometimes raised to dislike or distrust members of another. These are ingrained biases, nestled deep into the history of a group and a culture. They're often ancestral. There are some places where people from one neighbourhood are biased against those from another. People of particular countries have biases against those of specific others. This happens around the world over and over again.

One of the biggest problems
with the world today is that we
have large groups of people
who will accept whatever
they hear… just because
it suits their worldview.

NEIL **DE****GRASSE TYSON**

Look at the People in Your Life

Now that we've explored some of the typical sources of bias that may affect our behaviours and thought patterns, let's look a bit deeper at some of the bias in our own lives. Picture your closest friends, your significant other(s), your boss and your relatives – anyone you interact with often or have chosen to be a part of your life. Do most of these people fit in the same social groups as you? Do they all share the same race, religion and sexuality as you? This question can not only help you assess your own biases about who you choose to spend time with; it can also help you see the type of biases you may be exposed to in your social circles.

If the only people you're sharing ideas, stories and memories with are those who hold most of the same social identifiers and perspectives as you, you're missing out on experiencing so much of the diversity humanity has to offer.

For example, if you are a white, heterosexual Christian person (obviously you can swap these characteristics with any of you own) and you only spend time with other white, heterosexual Christians, when do you learn about the perspectives of people of other races, sexualities, religions and backgrounds? How do you become actively unbiased toward those groups without getting to know them?

Much of unconscious bias can be attributed to the way you spend your day-to-day life and the people you interact with. The neighbourhoods you walk through. Your colleagues. The restaurant workers who serve you. The passengers you sit next to on the train. While at times you cannot change the situation, there are many other occasions where you are making an unconscious decision about who you share your space with. Have you chosen to sit in a particular carriage of the train based on the people already there? Is there a reason why you sought the help of one customer assistant when there were others to choose from?

By acknowledging these patterns, you might help expose some of your unconscious biases.

One Thing Does Not Make a Person

Just as it can be harmful not to have any people in your life of differing backgrounds, races, sexualities, abilities and so on, if you label someone specifically by an aspect of their personal identity, this is also bias, and it's more than just unconscious: it's active and verbal. If you refer to someone as your "gay friend" or "lady doctor" or "Black professor" or "male nurse" – whatever the case may be – you're othering them and targeting an aspect of who they are, singling it out for notice. Often this is done for attention, to let other people know you have a friend of a different sexuality or race. Other times it's done as an identifier, to specify *which* doctor or friend or co-worker you're referring to. But ultimately, none of these things should be noteworthy identifiers. If the only way you're able to describe someone is by their race, gender, sexuality, religion, or another deeply personal part of their identity, think about why you may be doing so and how you can avoid generalizations like this in the future.

When Unconscious Bias Becomes Action

You may think that your unconscious mind doesn't control your actions, so your unconscious biases would be nothing more than internal, having no real-life effect. However, it's actually common for the biases you hold unconsciously to leak into your decisions, actions, way of speaking and manner of interacting with people. This is a common issue, and it's why bias has such an effect on how we live our lives. When each of us goes around, even just sometimes, intentionally or unintentionally stereotyping or being exclusionary or discriminatory, someone else is always on the receiving end of that negativity.

So, how can unconscious bias show up in your day-to-day actions? Here are a few signs:

- Changes in your eye contact, body language and facial expressions.

- Changes in the way you speak to someone and the language you use (for example, the complexity of the wording, the tone, how much time you spend on a conversation, how engaged you are).

- Changes to where you place yourself in a room or public space.

- Changes to how actively you listen to someone and how focused you are on them.

What Does It Mean That We're All Biased?

Does having unconscious bias automatically make you a bad person? Of course not. As mentioned earlier, it's safe to assume that everyone, even those who have already made great strides to undo their biases, occasionally experiences unconscious bias, or at least has in the past. It's ingrained in your brain, both due to complex psychology and years of reinforcement. It's a part of being human. It's also something that holds us back in so many ways. Bias can keep us from meeting or becoming close to people who could be amazing parts of our lives. It could make us judge someone and damage a relationship. It can hurt strangers. Over the course of many years, racism, sexism, homophobia and a host of other deeply harmful ideologies have also been the overwhelming result of bias, primarily conscious bias, though they are reinforced daily by our unconscious biases.

So, it is critical to recognize unconscious bias. And when it turns into action, subtle or major, it's important to notice and stop it.

Stereotypes and Bias

There is a bit of nuance to the difference between these two words and concepts, so let's dig a little deeper. The concept of bias should be clearer now, but how does a stereotype differ? Stereotypes are preconceived ideas ascribed to an entire group or set of people who share one thing in common (for example, a race, gender or sexuality).

Some stereotypes *feel* playful and harmless – for example, "white men can't dance" is a common joking stereotype. Nevertheless, no matter the playful intention, every stereotype does harm by grouping many people by one arbitrary and often inaccurate connection. Many other stereotypes are more clearly detrimental and hurtful, making large sweeping statements about the abilities or qualities of a massive group of people when each individual is a unique person.

Any stereotype can be harmful to someone. More importantly, stereotypes can cause and instil biases. If you hear a stereotype enough times, your brain will recall it in a moment of rapid decision-making or judgement. Even if you *think* you don't believe a stereotype, it may subtly influence decisions you make about who to hire, who to trust or who to date.

Understanding Preconceptions

Ever heard the phrase "preconceived notions"? This, too, has its connections to bias. Simply put, a preconceived notion or preconception is an opinion created without any evidence to support it. It's an idea you have before you gather any facts. Instead you form it based on assumptions, common sense, or, often, bias. Here's where they overlap.

Some preconceptions can be good ones, or at least safe ones. For instance, many women walking alone at night will assume *any* man approaching them is a potential threat. This is a preconceived notion, and it's sad that so many women have it, but it allows them to take precautions and stay safe.

Other times we have a preconception that we'll get along with someone or that we like someone. We're still assuming this before getting to know them, but it's in a positive way. However, it's the other times, when we assume something negative about someone, that our preconceptions are also bias, and that we need to note them and adjust them.

The Benefits of Diversity

It's simple to say that the immense diversity of humans makes our world better. But it's also helpful to go deeper and explore some of the reasons why.

In the workplace, diversity in a team provides more variety in ideas and in solutions and approaches to problems. A diverse team also provides better customer service, as they're able to better connect to customers or clients of a wider range of backgrounds. And when you're hiring from the most diverse pool possible, you have the best potential candidates. When you don't limit your hiring options by race, age or gender, you can hire the best of the best.

Similar benefits exist in diverse classrooms. Students learn more about backgrounds different from their own and become more accepting and aware as adults. There are more perspectives and opinions offered. This leads to better and more thought-provoking conversations, particularly with the right teacher or professor.

The benefits of diversity don't end there. The list goes on and on. Bias often limits us from accessing these benefits.

Empathy: Why Acceptance Is Good for Everyone

Empathy is the admirable ability to feel, understand or share the emotions of others. It's a respectable trait, and one that makes people more conscious and considerate members of the human race. When you are really able to feel what someone else could be feeling, putting yourself in their emotional shoes, it's hard to be biased toward them. If you recognize that someone feels the same range of emotions as you, that some days they struggle the same ways you do, it's difficult to still feel bias, prejudice and discrimination toward them.

This is why empathy heals. Acceptance heals. When you see another person, a stranger, and you make a conscious choice to assume only the best of them, you are being accepting. When you put yourself in their position and try to imagine their emotions, you're being empathetic. And when you're actively being empathetic or accepting, you can't be biased at the same time.

Summing Up

By now, hopefully it's clear that even though bias is a huge, pervasive issue and a complex topic, there are ways of breaking it down so that each of us can start to understand it, and thus eventually work to overcome it. Going forward, as you read the rest of the book, keep these basic points in mind:

- Bias is a universal issue. It's not something that just you, or just me, or just some of us have. All of us have some unconscious biases, even just occasional ones or passing thoughts. That's okay.

- Bias comes from many different sources. It could be caused by evolutionary instincts, the people in your life, social media, advertising, personal experiences, basic psychology or trauma. Or, more likely, it's a combination of those things.

- Becoming less biased is a matter of acknowledging and being more conscious about your reactions and thoughts.

- Diversity makes our world better, without question.

- When in doubt, choose acceptance and empathy. They leave no room for bias.

Chapter Two

BIAS IN SOCIETY

So how does bias look when it appears in our lives? How does it affect communities and real people? Where does bias appear most often around the world?

This chapter explores the most common biases that countries and communities around the world still experience daily. These are some of the groups of people most prone to being stereotyped, discriminated against, mistreated and pre-judged. We will explore some of the facts and statistics that go hand in hand with these global biases, along with some of the more subtle microaggressions that demonstrate our unconscious biases. We will also look at some of the parts of society where these common biases infiltrate and affect people's lives. For example, healthcare, education and workplaces are all major bias hotspots.

In the space of this book each section can only briefly cover topics that have filled many full-length books on their own. There is so much more information out there about topics such as racism, sexism and disability bias. Use this as a jumping-off point to start your education, but continue from there. For a list of further reading, see page 140–143.

"

You are not a statistic or a stereotype, so when they minimize you, dehumanize you, objectify you, you must push back with your whole weight.

"

CHANEL MILLER

THE WEIGHT OF BIAS MAY SEEM DAUNTING; LET IT BE MOTIVATING INSTEAD

Exploring Common Biases

There are countless things that create bias, and there are also countless biases. Some are ultra-specific and may tie directly in to an experience you had sometime in your life. Then there are the most common biases, the ones we see or experience daily or weekly in the news, on social media or in daily life. These may be biases people have against you. They may be ones you have against others. The pages to come will explore some of the most common biases, like race, gender, sexuality, disability, age and so on, in more depth.

But there are countless other biases you may encounter in your own self-exploration or in your encounters with other people. Here are some of the biases that won't be covered at length here but are still worth keeping in mind:

- Education
- Poverty/wealth
- Mental health/illness
- Citizenship status
- Home ownership
- Attractiveness
- Native language

- Political affiliation/ beliefs
- Relationship status or relationship style
- Family structure and background
- Accent
- Profession

Benevolent vs Hostile Prejudice

As we explore some of the common biases, it's also important to stay aware of different categorizations and terminology. One distinction that sometimes comes into play is that of benevolent versus hostile prejudice. This categorization was established in 1996 and primarily focused on the topic of sexism, though it has since been extended to other biases, including those of race, disability and age.

Benevolent prejudice:

- Essentially bias that appears positive or harmless on the surface but has the same result of placing groups in an inferior position. Bias in disguise.

- Often used to help justify hostile prejudices.

- Examples of benevolent prejudice include; stating that women are "just better at homemaking" or make "great secretaries"; saying that elderly people are all sweet but incompetent; seeing disabled people as vulnerable or needing supervision; viewing all gay men as fun and flamboyant; saying that Black people are athletic and musical.

Hostile prejudice:

- Classic prejudice as you picture it: derogatory language, discrimination, negative action, outward hatred.

- Can be applied to any group who faces bias.

Race and Racism

Among the many ways we as humans hurt each other through bias and discrimination, racism is easily the most pervasive and systemic. For as long as humans have gathered in groups and societies, people of different skin colours and races have harboured resentments and discrimination toward each other. This is an issue that has plagued us for thousands of years and many generations, yet it persists to this day. Bias toward people of other races continues to pull us apart. Rather than celebrating the beauty in our diversity and differences, racism damages so many communities of colour around the world.

Some of the darkest moments and periods in human history have stemmed from racism and racial bias. Think of slavery, civil wars, world wars, race riots and segregation. These things have not disappeared. And in our present-day world it's also plain to see racism and racial bias in smaller daily forms, in anything from derogatory language, to hiring discrimination, to police violence and beyond. No matter the place we live, there is racial bias all around us. It is a constant and often violent form of bias.

Why does racism exist?

This is a question that's been observed and studied from every possible perspective again and again. And there are plenty of theories out there for why we have bias toward people of other races. One reason is comfort. Naturally we feel more comfortable around people who are similar to us. There is considerable research supporting this claim. However, this instinct often results in the opposite feeling – discomfort or distrust toward people who are different from us. Something unfamiliar becomes something unpleasant.

Some psychologists also point to a theory of social dominance. This indicates that cultures all have hierarchies and that groups in power want to retain that power and level of dominance, both consciously and unconsciously. Thus bias persists as long as these power hierarchies do.

Though people from any group may experience racism, there are some groups who are especially vulnerable to intense racism and discrimination, according to the UN. These include:

- Women of colour
- People of colour also living in extreme poverty
- Migrants
- People of African descent
- Indigenous peoples
- National, ethnic, religious or linguistic minorities (who are also people of colour)

Around the World: Racism Facts and Figures

Speaking generally of the racism that exists throughout the world is a start, but going deeper into what this really looks like helps shed more light on how massive an issue racial bias really is. Here are a few examples of racism happening around the world:

- Police violence against Black people is not exclusive to the United States. For example, in Rio de Janeiro, Brazil, in 2018, 75 per cent of people killed by law enforcement were Black.

- Australia has a long history of racial discrimination against its indigenous people. Many subtly biased and racist government policies have been instated even in recent years.

- In a 2020 survey, 52 per cent of UK citizen respondents said the UK was either fairly racist or very racist as a society. In 2018 and 2019, there were over 16,000 racist incidents and crimes reported by police in London alone.

- As of 2019, there were an estimated 940 active "hate groups" across the United States. The majority, though not all, were racially motivated.

Racist Microaggressions

One of the most common manifestations of unconscious racial bias is not large-scale demonstrative discrimination, but rather the more subtle, hidden and sometimes "well-intentioned" comments, questions and actions. These are termed "microaggressions".

At first glance, they're seemingly "positive". But the result is still othering, belittling or offending someone of another race or group. It just may not be as noticeable or obvious.

This could look like:

- **Asking someone of another race about their hair or touching it.**

- **Zeroing in on one race in talks of social justice and leaving out other people of colour (for example, holding a diversity workshop and using only examples about Black people, making people of other races still feel left out).**

- **Praising someone of colour on being "articulate" or having impressive speaking skills, insinuating this is unexpected.**

- **Mistaking one person you work with for another person of their race and addressing them by the wrong name.**

While most of us would never consciously consider ourselves racist, we need to be aware that micro-aggressions like these are deeply ingrained in our thought patterns and can surface without us realizing, unless we actively work to avoid them.

Gender, Identity and Sexuality

Another of the largest and most pervasive biases is bias toward women and female-presenting people, referred to more commonly as sexism. It's another problem that spans all of human history. This doesn't mean there aren't people or places who hold conscious or unconscious biases toward men or male-presenting people. In many of those cases, biases are often rooted in personal, *individual* experience or traumas, as opposed to the deep historical and societal basis that forms the more common bias against women.

According to a survey conducted by the UN, approximately 90 per cent of people worldwide have some type of bias against women. This survey included questions about whether women, in comparison to men, are equally powerful political leaders and business executives, among other things.

Additionally, in more recent decades as the LGBTQ+ (Lesbian, Gay, Bisexual, Transgender, Queer and others) community have felt more empowered to embody their true gender expressions, some new gender identities have become more a part of the mainstream social conversation and awareness. These include genderqueer, non-binary and agender, though there are others. People with these identities also face higher than average levels of bias and discrimination for their gender.

What are some roots of sexism and gender bias?

Across the world, women are living under levels of oppression. In much of Europe, North America and other Western countries, this presents itself in the form of sexist lawmaking, harassment, assault, workplace issues, misrepresentation or lack of representation and double standards. In a number of of other countries, women still have no rights whatsoever; the bias is so deep that women are killed over perceived crimes or minor infractions.

Bias against women can be traced back to the oldest human records. In many places, religious texts indicated male dominance over women and thus dictated the ways that societies and cultures were built. Additionally, many societies of the past, reliant on hard labour for most of the economy, put more stock in the perceived greater physical abilities of men, and the result were male-led communities.

Much of the strength of gender bias comes from repetition over time. Repetition of male figures in power has become comfortable and normal to people, to the point that picturing female leaders goes against the grain and bias is reinforced. Breaking this pattern starts with the simple step of recognizing our unconscious biases and undoing them.

How Does Sexism Affect Us?

Around the world there are countless ways that women, girls and female-presenting people are affected by gender bias. Some are small things people get used to and accept as a normal part of life. Others are startling statistics that seem out of place in a world where we talk so much about equality. Here are a few results of gender bias and sexism:

- Women are accustomed to catcalling and harassment, no matter the country.

- On average, depending on the country, women make 10–50 per cent less money than their male counterparts. This percentage is often higher for older women or women of colour, even in countries with fairly low wage gaps.

- Women are generally under-represented in high-ranking and executive positions.

- Only 38 per cent of the world's countries have had a female leader in the past 50 years. There are currently only 23 female leaders out of 146 countries whose leadership is tracked.

- In 104 countries there are many jobs that women are legally prohibited to do. This affects the employment choices of an estimated 2.7 billion women.

- On average, women do approximately twice as much unpaid work as men.

- Approximately 35 per cent of women worldwide have experienced physical or sexual violence by a partner, according to the WHO.

Sexuality

Throughout history, people who are non-heterosexual or non-cisgender (they don't identify with the gender they were assigned at birth) have faced massive discrimination and violence. Due to this bias, hiding and disguising their true identities and preferences was (and in many places and cultures still is) commonplace. But as some parts of the world have begun to progress and show more acceptance for the LGBTQ+ community, more members have felt able to express themselves for who they love, who they're attracted to, their gender expressions and their preferences.

Still, there is a great deal of bias in our society toward members of the LGBTQ+ community. Homophobia, perhaps an overly general term, refers to bias and prejudice against anyone who is or is perceived as gay, lesbian, bisexual, transgender, pansexual, asexual or another member of the queer community. As with many of the other groups who face deeply rooted bias, like people of colour and women, the bias experienced by non-heterosexual and non-cisgender people leads to a host of painful consequences. This includes violence, suicides and homicides (particularly in the trans community), workplace and hiring discrimination, healthcare discrimination and laws limiting basic human rights.

Legal and Criminal Bias Against the LGBTQ+ Community

There are many painful real-world results of bias faced by members of the queer community. One of the largest comes straight from the top: government. Governments around the world have let bias and discrimination cloud the lives of LGBTQ+ people for centuries. Here are a few current examples:

- In the United States, same sex marriage was only legalized nationwide in 2015.

- Same-sex marriage is currently only legal in 29 of 195 countries in the world.

- At least 70 countries have laws that criminalize same-sex relations. Some countries do little to enforce these laws, while others punish people with fines, jail time and in some places the death penalty.

- In the Central African Republic, a criminal code includes punishments for same-sex conduct in public, though heterosexual conduct in public is acceptable.

- Many laws around the world criminalize or ban transgender and non-binary people from using public facilities like restrooms, restrict them from sports participation and make it difficult or impossible for them to get proper identification documents, among other things.

Everyday Gender Microaggressions

Women, female-presenting people and members of the transgender community experience myriad microaggressions every day.

For example, transgender people often hear things like "But you don't look transgender!" While the perpetrator thinks they're being complimentary, this comment is in fact often hurtful. Those in the trans community say comments like this make it seem like "looking trans" is undesirable – that their ultimate goal should be to look as binary and cisgender as possible – when really they just want to look however their personal expression and style dictates.

For women, other comments and behaviours are common. These often fall under the scope of "benevolent prejudices", as do many microaggressions. Here are a few of the most prevalent:

- People assuming that women in high-status positions have lower rank/status than they actually do.

- Being frequently interrupted by men who want to explain something "better".

- Use of only the "he" pronoun in workplace documents, books, legal texts and so on.

- People being surprised when women over a certain age aren't married, don't have kids or don't want kids.

Age and Ageism

Ageism, a term coined in 1969, refers typically to bias and discrimination against people of older ages and includes:

- Prejudice against seniors and elderly people.
- Fear and prejudice surrounding old age and death.
- Discriminatory actions and behaviours toward older people.
- Institutional policies and procedures that encourage stereotypes about old age and seniors.

This term has also been used conversely to refer to bias and prejudice against young people and young adults, who have at times been denied rights or respect due to appearing too young or the perception that young people aren't "mature enough" to handle aspects of adult life. Either way you look at it, age-based bias is another example of bias that results in hurtful real-world action and discrimination.

When it comes to ageism toward older people, a common cause seems to be fear of death and ageing. Due to the fact that so many of us hold such negative and fearful associations with the end of life, some of us naturally associate old age with these unpleasant feelings, building an unconscious bias against the elderly.

What Are Some Tangible Results of Ageism?

As always, knowing a bias exists is one thing, but seeing some facts and figures about how it appears in our society puts it into perspective. While some cultures revere and respect their elderly citizens and the ageing process, others look down upon it.

Remember, ageism can also mean discrimination against younger generations, which also does harm. But here are some real-world examples of bias against older people:

- In the United States three in five older workers have experienced age-based discrimination in their workplace. Studies found that 76 per cent see age as an obstacle in finding a new or better job, and about half of older workers are prematurely pushed out of jobs.

- Research suggests that elderly people with a negative outlook on ageing could live 7.5 years less than those who are positive about their age.

- When surveyed, only 26 per cent of the general population viewed people over 70 as "capable". Instead, older people are often viewed as kind and friendly but incompetent and pitiable. This is an example of benevolent prejudice.

Size and Appearance

A concept known as sizeism or size discrimination is also common, especially in our current age of social media, which is a breeding ground for unreasonable beauty standards. There is a common bias against people deemed overweight or underweight, based mostly on a perception that the person is "unhealthy".

When you feel bias against a stranger or acquaintance based on their size, you likely don't know anything about their health. Perhaps they have a medical condition that affects their weight. Maybe they're at a perfectly healthy weight for their personal needs, body type and fitness. And most importantly, maybe they're completely happy in their body and don't have any interest in your negative perception of them or their "health" issues. It's been shown many times that weight bias actually harms a person's health, both physical and mental.

When so much of our society has an ingrained belief that beauty only comes in a particular size and body type, we lose sight of the fact that *every* body is beautiful and valuable. The internet provides images that we consider "goals", even though more often than not they're retouched or edited beyond recognition.

Denying people access
to value is an incredibly
insidious form of emotional
violence, one that our culture
wields aggressively and
liberally to keep marginalized
groups small and quiet.

LINDY WEST

Disability Bias

The word *disability* in itself covers a wide and ever-evolving range of things. In essence, a disability is any type of physical, emotional or mental limitation that has an effect on how someone lives their life. Physical disabilities can include anything from an amputated limb to a chronic pain condition or cerebral palsy, with a range of other conditions in between. Mental and emotional disabilities are sometimes harder to define or exist on more of a spectrum, including things like autism spectrum disorder, Down syndrome, schizophrenia and general developmental disabilities. Some disabilities are acquired during life, while others exist from birth. Regardless, it's estimated that about 15 per cent of the global population, well over one billion people, lives with one or more disabilities.

Yet it's one of the more uncomfortable things for people to talk about. A huge percentage of people don't feel comfortable meeting and speaking to someone with a mental or cognitive disability. Many people avoid interactions with people who are mentally or physically disabled, due to their own fear. For this large portion of our worldwide population, bias often leads to avoidance and neglect.

What issues do disabled people face due to bias?

As with any group facing serious bias, disabled people around the world see real-life consequences of discrimination every day. This varies greatly from country to country. There are places with substantial supports in place. Even in those countries, unconscious bias exists. In other places, people with disabilities face extreme prejudice and difficulty getting any type of services. Here are some examples of how this manifests around the world:

- In Latin America it is estimated that only 20–30 per cent of children with disabilities are educated.

- In 2014, 10 per cent of UN members guaranteed the right to health for people with disabilities, because the lack of it was so pervasive.

- In the US, where the average yearly income is around $34,000, half of people with disabilities earn $15,000 or less per annum. Across the globe, people with disabilities are far more likely to be impoverished.

- Consistently, studies done around the world have found that large percentages of disabled people have needs going unmet, including needs for healthcare and medication, support services, financial help and technical devices like assistive communication tools, mobility aids and wheelchairs.

Faith and Religion

Religious discrimination and persecution has been around since the birth of organized religions many thousands of years ago. As soon as multiple differing faiths developed there were people threatened by the existence of a religious belief other than their own. Religious differences and persecutions have been the cause of innumerable wars over countless generations, and these devastating religious conflicts continue in parts of the world today.

In its most extreme forms, religious bias becomes religious persecution, which in some times and places has led to people being executed for their beliefs. Nearly every religion has been persecuted at one point or another in history, and there are biases out there toward every religion on earth. Some religions, as a group, are collectively trained to feel bias or contempt toward another, one perceived as contradictory, offensive or heretical to their own.

To this day, religious bigotry and bias frequently leads to violence, attacks on places of worship, derogatory language and hate crimes.

Though most faiths and their members seek love and peace, some members of varied faiths do still feel discrimination or bias towards other groups, sometimes based on the teachings of their faith.

In history (a few examples):

- Jewish people have been persecuted many times over, including by ancient Romans and Greeks, Christians, Muslims, Nazis, Imperial-era Russians and others.

- In the early days of the faith, Muslims were persecuted by Meccans. Persecution has continued by other groups throughout history.

- Hindus were persecuted by Muslim rulers and European colonialists.

- Buddhists have often been persecuted, including by twentieth-century communist parties.

Today (a few examples):

- Currently, Muslims face restrictions in a total of 142 countries and are among the most persecuted groups in the world.

- There are currently 13 countries in the world where you can be sentenced to death for atheism.

- As of 2015, more than 97 per cent of Jews, Muslims and Hindus lived in countries where persecution and open discrimination occurred.

Nationality Bias and Xenophobia

Xenophobia is a fear or hatred of strangers and people from other countries. In general it's connected to a bias toward people of other nationalities, though the two concepts can also deviate. Xenophobia is generally an extreme discrimination, whereas nationality bias may be a more vaguely unconscious bias against someone from a specific country or foreign people in general. This can stem from fear of the unknown, but it's very often connected to racial bias, as well as language bias and others. So, as is often the case, this may be a bias that is naturally wrapped up in other biases.

Nationality bias is seen often in the United States. This is shown in the strong anti-immigrant bias displayed by many of its citizens, often specifically toward people from Mexico and Latin America. But it's not alone in this. Generally, every country's citizens have a natural bias against people from another country, often a neighbouring nation. This often appears as a general distrust and dislike, but in some some cases it veers into active discrimination, violence and wars, a tragic escalation that has happened throughout history and continues in some areas today.

Bias in Action

Having explored some of the most common forms of bias, we'll look more closely at some of the parts of life and society where bias and discrimination show themselves most clearly and where their effects are felt most strongly for disadvantaged groups.

Due to the fact that biases and decision-making patterns – even though they can be undone – it's hard for them not to take hold in the world. If you ever change your tone of voice or language based on the person you're talking to, you've shown bias in real life.

And if you've ever received less accurate medical care because of part of your identity, or been targeted by harassment or discrimination of any kind, you've felt the real-world effects of bias too. It's all around us. By learning more about bias in action we can become more empowered to stand up against injustices when we see them happening around us.

Bias in Derogatory Language

One of the most noticeable and simple ways bias shows itself is in derogatory and discriminatory language. Without having to include a list of offensive terminology, I'm certain you can think for a moment and come up with plenty of examples of racist, homophobic, sexist and other derogatory words and phrases that hurt groups of people. We know these words, and many of them have been removed from "acceptable" vocabulary, but that doesn't mean people stop using them and even directing them toward others with the intention of offending.

As time goes on, more words enter this realm of offensive language. We realize that the things we're saying have roots or secondary meanings that actually cause harm. For example, calling someone "crazy" is something we should rethink and avoid. It actually relates back to mental health and hurts or discriminates against those dealing with real mental illnesses.

Making changes to your language can be tough, especially if you're accustomed to speaking a certain way. However, biased and offensive language perpetuates harm against marginalized groups, and avoiding those words in your own vocabulary is the easiest way to make an impact.

Bias in Choosing Neighbourhoods and Schools

Bias also appears in the way people choose where to live, which says a lot about their unconscious biases. People often avoid neighbourhoods and towns they deem "unsafe" or "loud", which often has to do with nothing more than unconscious bias against immigrants or people of other races.

In many countries, neighbourhoods with higher immigrant populations have ended up attracting larger and larger proportions of immigrant residents. This is due to a combination of people wanting to congregate with those who are similar them, and the concentration of more affordable housing being accessible to lower-income groups.

Similarly, a concept called "white flight" has been long studied in the United States and other areas. This is an ethnic segregation in neighbourhoods caused by white people "fleeing" those neighbourhoods as more people of colour move in. This accelerates a neighbourhood's transition into being seen as a "Black" or otherwise diverse neighbourhood and further establishes a lack of white residents moving in. The bias becomes ingrained over decades and affects the way new generations view the neighbourhoods, ensuring the bias remains strong and unconscious.

Bias in Education

When it comes to education bias, issues arise in every country and across every age group. Here are some examples:

- Unconscious bias on the part of educators often leads to learning inequities and disparities for students of colour, female students, disabled students and other groups that are often discriminated against.

- White teachers in the United States were 40 per cent less likely to predict their Black students would successfully complete four-year degrees.

- Whitewashing (deliberately concealing unpleasant or incriminating facts) and selective censorship of material is common in widely used school textbooks in the United States and elsewhere.

- In 2018 in London, England, it was found that the primary school attainment averages for Black/Caribbean students was 17 per cent behind that of white students due to bias in discipline and work assessment.

"

I think unconscious bias is one
of the hardest things to get at.

RUTH BADER GINSBURG

Bias in Healthcare

When it comes to your personal health, you want to be able to get the care you need without problems, judgement or bias, right? That should be a basic expectation in life. Yet so many groups face some form of bias in either receiving enough care, or qualified and unbiased care. Racism, sexism, transphobia, ableism and homophobia all play a part in the world of healthcare, and it means that too often people find themselves struggling with health issues, without reliable medical professionals or medical care that they can trust.

Time and time again studies have proven that racial and ethnic minorities and women generally receive fewer treatment options, less accurate diagnoses, reduced pain management and have worse overall outcomes from medical treatment. Similarly, LGBTQ+ people, particularly transgender individuals, often struggle to get unbiased care, especially for things like transition surgery and hormone treatment.

Bias also goes the other way in healthcare. It's not at all uncommon for patients to be mistrusting of Black, minority or female doctors. Doctors of colour have often experienced patients requesting that other providers take over their care.

Facts and figures

This is a small glimpse at what healthcare bias looks like around the world:

- False information and racial stereotyping can lead to improper care for minorities in the United States and other countries.

- People with disabilities, many of whom need more than average healthcare, report needs being unmet around the world. According to the WHO, recent surveys of people with serious mental disorders reported that about 35–50 per cent in developed countries and 76–85 per cent in developing countries received no treatment in the year prior.

- In the United States, Black, American Indian and Alaska Native women are two to three times more likely to die from childbirth than white women, due to racist barriers to medical care and biased medical notions.

- Access to female reproductive care, abortion and contraceptives is frequently limited or banned around the world, including in developed countries.

- Medical care or procedures that go against religious views are often carried out despite requests for other options.

Bias in Criminal Justice

The United States' criminal justice system is the largest and most well-known in the world, and its overt and historical bias is also fairly common knowledge. It is far from the only country with biased policing, sentencing or prison systems, though. In many countries, unfair and discriminatory laws and practices lead to harsh sentences for things that many of us in other parts of the world think of as commonplace – same-sex relationships, gender expression, contraception and freedom of religion, for example.

Bias certainly exposes itself in the context of justice and prison. In the United States it's still not unheard of for two people to be convicted of the same crime in the same city with the same past record and receive wildly different prison sentences. The only clear difference between them? Their race. While occurrences like this have decreased over time, it's a historical issue that still exists. And many of its past victims – non-violent drug offenders of colour, for example – are still serving decades-long sentences, while violent white criminals received comparably mild sentences and have since gone free.

Consistently, beyond the United States, people of racial and ethnic minorities are stopped more often by police, pulled over more often for no reason, arrested more frequently and convicted more often. They are given stricter sentences for similar crimes.

This is due to law enforcement bias, witness bias, jury bias and system bias. Every country is different, and in each one bias is exposed in unique ways. Sometimes there is a distinct lack of willingness to believe female victims or defendants. Elsewhere its imposing a harsher sentence on someone perceived to be poor or uneducated or a religious or ethnic minority.

Studies in recent years by the European Network Against Racism found prevalent institutional racism in all aspects of the justice system in the EU. This included a police tendency to take reports of racially motivated crimes less seriously. In other situations, racially based crimes would no longer mention the racial element once in the court setting. Lithuania, for example, doesn't even recognize the concept of "hate crime". All of this was discovered despite substantial evidence that racially based and anti-semitic crimes are on the rise across Europe.

Bias in the Workplace

If you Google the word "bias", you'll find "workplace" is one of the top keywords you'll see over and over. It's an environment where bias is often most prevalent and noticeable. Workplace harassment is extremely commonplace, and this is bias plain and simple. Hiring and firing is often steeped in discrimination. Promotions and pay raises tend to favour those who are male or non-minorities.

This is not to say that every company in every country is a racist, sexist, harassment-fuelled workplace of bias. Of course not. But overwhelmingly, most companies have some issues, simply because all people have biases, conscious or unconscious, and those affect how we deal with others. Put a few people, or a dozen people, or a thousand people together in an office and on a team and those many competing biases will come into play. The results are discriminatory and challenging.

At a glance

- More than 50 per cent of women worldwide report having been sexually harassed at work. In male-dominated industries the figures are higher. An estimated 75 per cent of people who spoke up about workplace harassment faced retaliation after reporting. A predicted 75 per cent of harassment incidents are completely unreported.

- Bias-based workplace bullying and harassment is also incredibly common. Men report less sexual harassment but more assaults and thefts. Racism is often a factor, with minorities facing greater harassment and derogatory language.

- The transgender community faces double the normal rate of unemployment. More than one in four transgender people has lost a job due to suspected bias.

- Approximately half of LGBTQ+ employees in the United States choose to remain closeted at work.

- As of 2020, the global percentage of women in senior management roles was 29 per cent.

- Throughout Europe bias against the Roma people has led to unemployment rates of 50–90 per cent, depending on the area, and extreme levels of poverty.

- In the UK, young adults report more ageism against them in the workplace than those in their 50s.

- Across Europe, a person with a "moderate" disability has a 47 per cent chance of being employed; for someone with a "severe" disability this falls to 25 per cent.

Hiring Discrimination

Ideally, what factors would determine if someone got a job or an interview? Their qualifications and ability to do the job well? Unfortunately, unconscious bias can be so ingrained that many interview and hiring decisions are unknowingly influenced by the hiring manager or team's personal biases.

Many forms of bias are actually unique to hiring. For example, *expectation anchor bias*. In this situation, someone gets attached to one piece of information about someone – their college, the fact that they're very similar to the role's predecessor – and then disregard other candidates almost immediately. Another is called *similarity attraction bias*. Here, hiring teams seek out candidates and qualities that match themselves. For example, a primarily male hiring team will almost never hire a female candidate, and a white hiring team will lean toward white candidates.

Another startling statistic: in studies done in recent years in the United States, job applicants with "white-sounding" names received 50 per cent more interview requests than those with "stereotypically Black" or ethnic names. The same has gone for any "ethnic-sounding" names elsewhere as well, including Canada, the UK, France and other parts of Europe.

We won't unlock the full
potential of the workplace
until we see how far from
equality we really are.

SHERYL SANDBERG

Chapter Three

BECOMING CONSCIOUSLY UNBIASED

From the basic foundation of knowledge you've now hopefully built about bias and its mark on the world, the next and most important step is your own personal journey. It's important to understand as much as you can about how bias works if you want to be able to find it in your own subconscious and actively oppose it.

In this chapter, you'll find numerous thought exercises, prompts for self-reflection and techniques to help you reveal your own unconscious biases and reframe them in order to become more consciously unbiased. You will also have the chance to dive into some of the self-biases that may be holding you back, whether from your full potential or from self-love.

And then you'll practise. Questioning yourself, journaling and doing visualization exercises all help to build and cement the skills to spot bias in yourself and others and then learn to do something about it.

Continue your self-empowerment journey and choose to live without bias holding you back.

"Have a bias toward action –
let's see something happen
now. You can break that big
plan into small steps and take
the first step right away.

INDIRA GANDHI

FACE THE JOURNEY HEAD-ON, AND DIVE IN — THERE IS NO BETTER TIME

The First Key to Progress:
An Open and Engaged Mind

Before we dive into the myriad ways to identify your unconscious biases, address them and actively uncouple from them with thought exercises and self-questioning, there's one essential component to be aware of. In order for any of this chapter to be effective, you have to go into it with an open mind.

You will have to question yourself; you'll have to question moments in your past and thoughts that you have that may be difficult to accept and may make you uncomfortable. Exploring your biases is not about self-judgement; remember, everyone has unconscious bias. By doing the work of learning about biases, uncovering your own, acknowledging them and actively undoing them, you're committing to huge personal growth.

So, when you think you're ready to move into this chapter, you also have to be ready to engage with the prompts, think critically about the questions posed, delve into the exercises fully and truly keep your mind open to learning something new about yourself and your world.

Four Ways to Identify Your Unconscious Biases

Of course, there are far more than four ways to discover your own unconscious biases. You may try these things and realize they're not working for you and you need to get creative and try your own methods. But here are some places to start.

1 Get educated

Reading this book is a great start, since it provides an overview on bias as a whole, and some statistics and details to inform you. But it doesn't aim to be comprehensive, as this is a deeply complex and involved topic with so much to explore. There are countless other books and articles out there that study specific topics at more length.

So, think back. As you read the prior sections, were there any pieces of information that struck a particular chord with you? Is it because you were reading about a form of bias that affects you personally? Or was it possibly a source of bias or an effect you hadn't considered? These are places where you should dig deeper and explore your possible biases. Get online and read more; see what you learn about yourself.

2 Be mindful and practise self-awareness

While you are in the process of uncovering your unconscious biases, push yourself to go above and beyond in your self-awareness. We are very accustomed to ignoring most of our passing thoughts and only focusing on the ones that are recurring or force us to make decisions. Take some time, even just a portion of each day, to pay attention to as many of your individual thoughts as you can. This is particularly helpful to do when you're in a setting where you will be seeing and interacting with a variety of people – walking around town, getting food, at work, at an event or a party, and so on.

Rather than mindlessly letting bias infiltrate your casual thought patterns, focus on your instincts and thoughts that pass by. You don't even have to try to change them or adjust them; that's a step for later. Just make note of anything that feels like a sign of unconscious bias. Practise mindfulness and thought awareness whenever you can, especially until you've isolated some unconscious biases that you want to work on.

3   Have conversations

It may be hard to do all this unconscious bias investigation entirely on your own. While it *is* a personal growth journey and an internal exploration, having conversations with other people is an essential part of both realizing your biases and working to overcome them.

Some of these should be conversations with people you already know well and trust. Talk to them about your desire to pinpoint unconscious biases and explore some of the things you've learned from this book or your other research. They may very likely raise other points you hadn't considered. They may also remember past experiences that indicated bias, things you may have forgotten.

Then try to talk to other people. A co-worker, an acquaintance, a neighbour, a stranger at a cafe, a friend of a friend or anyone else. Ideally, try to talk to people who have some identities that differ from yours – a different sexual orientation, gender expression, race, religion, age, disability and so on. Broach the topic of bias openly and see if they have thoughts that can help you learn something about yourself or your bias journey.

4 Take implicit bias tests online

If you're looking for a more straightforward approach to uncovering some of your possible unconscious biases, you can take an implicit bias test online. These tests, put together by universities and research groups, ask a series of commonplace questions or have you select or match words and images. They keep things as subtle as possible; the questions aren't all as straightforward as "Would you prefer a male or female doctor?" Instead, they probe deeper and use psychological tools to determine subtleties in your preferences, as well as record how long it takes for you to answer certain questions. At the end they offer up potential implicit biases that your answers point to and even indicate how strong your biases may be toward that group or identity.

Far and away the most popular test, which is commonly used in training workshops and offices, is Project Implicit. This test was founded by a small group of scientists in 1998 and has expanded into a large non-profit organization and research group. You can find more about this test and others in the further reading section at the back of this book.

Uncovering Self-Biases
and Stereotypes

You've taken the time to observe your thoughts and actions and discover some of the unconscious biases you may have toward other people. This is a huge first step in becoming more consciously unbiased. But there's one other form of unconscious bias you may still be unaware of: bias toward yourself. Yes, it's absolutely possible to be biased toward a group that you're a part of or to feel bias about an identity you claim. These biases can form due to societal reinforcements over time – perhaps that you don't have the "perfect" body, or that someone of your race or gender or ability level can't do a particular job or achieve a particular goal.

Self-biases are also deeply detrimental, though instead of affecting the people you interact with, they affect you internally – your mental health, self-esteem and confidence to push for bigger and better things. If you believe that something about you makes you unworthy of a raise or not good enough for your dream job or ideal relationship, it's critical to assess the self-bias that's holding you back and overcome it.

Three Small Ways to Turn Self-Bias into Self-Love

As you have learned in this book and hopefully observed in your life, self-biases are harmful, just like any others. Conversely, self-love is healing and powerful.

Here are a few things you can try to to help you build more self-confidence:

1 **Catch yourself and question it.** Just as you do with unconscious bias you feel toward other people, if you find yourself thinking something negative about yourself, shut that down and question why you're thinking that way. Is it because the thought is true or because you've been influenced by social media, society, people in your life and so on?

2 **Purposely start or end the day with positive self-commentary.** Make a point of waking up and saying something kind to yourself. List off a few of the things you like about you. End the day the same way. Or do this every time you start to self-doubt.

3 **Treat yourself like you would your best friend.** If you'd never be biased or judgemental toward your best friend, act the same way with yourself. You deserve the same treatment.

Journaling Exercise: Mapping Your Unconscious Biases

Hopefully, using a combination of the methods from the past several pages, along with any personal investigating and other techniques of your own, you've come to realizations about some unconscious biases you have. Whether you notice it or not, these biases affect the interactions you have, the connections you make, your decisions, conversations and perceptions. Breaking past them is a challenge, but it's a worthwhile goal. Before moving on to steps and methods for overcoming biases, take some time to pull out a journal and write down any unconscious biases or self-biases you've discovered. You can always add more to this list as you learn more or progress through the various exercises ahead.

Remember: There is no judgement here. As always, this is a space for personal reflection and learning more about yourself.

Eight Steps to Being More Actively Unbiased

Now that you've identified and noted some of the unconscious biases you hold, you're ready to start working to undo and move past them. Even if some remnants of bias will always linger in your subconscious mind, you can make active choices to be unbiased in your thoughts, your actions, your decisions and your words. Over time these *conscious* choices to be unbiased will also help you reduce the recurrences of your *unconscious* biases.

There are plenty of other ways to become more consciously unbiased, but this is a great outline. Take it step by step. This is a big journey and things won't change overnight.

Step 1: Commit to the change and the time

If you're going to succeed at freeing yourself from unconscious biases and living a more unbiased life, commitment to working at the process over time is necessary. This is not a "one and done" plan. You can't undo years of reinforced societal unconscious bias by doing a little reading and a bit of thinking. It will take work and time and dedication to self-improvement.

Step 2: Acknowledge all your biased thoughts and question them

As mentioned before, this requires extra focus on your thoughts and reactions. Now that you've noted some of your biases, you should be able to hone in a bit when you're in public or interacting with people. When you notice a biased thought or instinct slip in, don't beat yourself up. Instead acknowledge it. Then question it. Why are you having this reaction to this person or situation? Is it a justified reaction? Do you have evidence to feel this way or are you making assumptions based on bias? Question everything; you should eventually start to learn more about the basis of your bias and how to break it.

Step 3: Reframe and reshape biased thoughts in the moment

After you question yourself, if you decide the thought or judgement definitely came from a place of unconscious bias and not the facts in front of you, reshape the thought into a positive one. Reconsider a negative assumption you made about someone and make a positive one instead. Mentally praise someone for their admirable accomplishment rather than being surprised by it.

Step 4: Adjust your perspective

If you feel an instinct to think poorly of someone, distrust them, judge them or dismiss them due to a bias, take a moment to create a positive story for them and realize that they have interests, feelings and emotions just like you. Even if they're a stranger, consider what kind of life they might have. Don't make negative assumptions, but try to give them the benefit of the doubt or see the best in them first. Instead of focusing on one part of their identity that you associate negatively, maybe think to yourself: "Are they married? Do they have kids? A close group of friends? What kind of things might they do for fun? How might they be struggling emotionally right now?" The person you're judging or making assumptions about may have more in common with you than you think. And though you may never know the answers to these questions, taking time to picture someone among loved ones, pursuing a favourite hobby or dealing with mental health issues can help you see that they're just another human trying to get by.

Step 5: Assess your first impressions

When you meet someone, mentally separate them from any group they may be associated with. Learn something about them as a person and use that as the foundation on which you build an opinion. When forming a first impression about someone, their race, gender, sexuality, religion, weight or age should not be a factor. Instead, intentionally assess someone's personality, their honesty and conversation style, their hobbies and interests, their stories. Base your impression of someone on the things that make them an individual, not the things that make them part of a large social group. Those are parts of their identity, but they're not what decides if they're a person worth getting to know better.

Step 6: Think before speaking

If you've identified a situation where you may act or speak with bias, take extra caution to speak slowly and consider the things you say before saying them. Make sure whatever you're about to say to someone is something that wouldn't offend you if you were in their position. This is always a good rule of thumb.

Step 7: Build a more diverse community in your life

This doesn't mean ditch the people who are too similar to you, and it also doesn't mean choose new friends based only on whether they have different backgrounds than you – that's another form of bias.

What it means is be genuinely open to welcoming new people into your life. People you socialize with don't have to be the same age as you. They don't have to have the same sexual orientation or religion or race. This doesn't only apply to friends. Talk to new people in your workplace. Connect with a neighbour or someone who goes to the same cafe. Open yourself up to a wider diversity of perspectives.

Step 8: Hold yourself (and others) accountable

The people who are closest to you should know about your goal to become more unbiased. Request that if they notice you slip up and make a comment or assumption based on bias they call you on it. It helps to have people you trust who can help you catch yourself. Let them know you'll always hear feedback without getting upset.

Exercise:
Questioning and Reframing Practice

One of the key steps to conquering a bias is being able to acknowledge a thought as it occurs in the moment, question it and then effectively reframe it, turning it on its head. So let's try that out with a question and answer exercise to practise reshaping a biased thought into an unbiased one instead.

Use the following blank pages to note down your answers to the following exercise, as well as the questions and reflections that come out of it.

First, choose one unconscious bias of your own. What is a simple scenario in your daily life where this bias could come into play? (For example, at a restaurant, in the office, at a party, walking down the street, at the doctor and so on.)

Write down a one-sentence thought you could have in this scenario that is bias-based. If possible, use an example of a thought you have actually had.

Now write out any questions you would ask yourself after acknowledging this biased thought.

From there, reframe the thought from one of bias, judgement and assumption to something positive. How would you recreate that thought in a way that is free of bias?

Exercise Notes

....

....

....

....

....

....

....

....

....

....

....

....

....

....

How Can You Avoid Microaggressions?

You've seen from some of the examples in chapter two just how simple and subtle microaggressions can appear. So how can you avoid being the perpetrator of biased microaggressive comments, questions and behaviours?

First, be more mindful of the words you say and the way you act. As has been mentioned before, learning to be less biased starts with paying attention to your thoughts, feelings, words and actions. Most microaggressive biased comments are things that just didn't need to be said in the first place. So before speaking, think about the comment and whether it expresses a bias or could indicate assumptions or stereotypes about the person you're speaking to. Want to compliment a person of colour on their hair? Reassess. Compliment their outfit or makeup skills or something not related to their race instead.

Do you ever change your tone of voice, the words you use or your body language based on the type of person you're interacting with? Why? Make a conscious effort to avoid these subtle expressions of bias.

Common Microaggressive Comments You May Not Realize Show Your Bias

Have you ever said one of these things? Or had them said to you? These are incredibly common microaggressive statements and questions that are a normal part of daily conversations. Before you say one of these things, pause, acknowledge your bias and choose to say nothing or something that isn't targeting someone's personal identities.

- Your hair is so beautiful. Your skin is so beautiful. Is that your natural hair?

- Your name is so hard to pronounce.

- The way you've handled your disability is so inspiring.

- You're really impressive for someone your age.

- Oh, you're gay/bisexual/lesbian/trans? So is my friend! You should meet them!

- I can't believe how eloquent you are.

- You speak such good English.

- I'm not racist, I have Black friends.

- You people...

- I don't see race.

- You're being crazy. She's so crazy.

- Are you still in school? You look so young!

Hidden Bias in Everyday Conversations

Many times our unconscious bias doesn't appear in the form of large-scale discrimination. Most commonly implicit bias shows up in subtler ways.

Here are three examples of possible conversations you could have with a friend, co-worker or relative on any given day. These are normal things to talk about and the responses are similar to things you've probably heard or said. They're also examples of unconscious bias appearing in the form of casual conversational assumptions.

PERSON 1: "I'm seeing a new doctor."
PERSON 2: "Nice, did you like him?"
PERSON 1: "Actually, she's a woman."

‣ *What bias was revealed?*

PERSON 1: "I went to my college friend Gina's wedding this weekend. I had a great time."
PERSON 2: "That's awesome. Are you friends with her husband too?"
PERSON 1: "Her wife, actually. But yes, we're pretty close!"

‣ *What bias was revealed?*

PERSON 1: "I'm so excited, I'm going to meet my friend's baby on Sunday."
PERSON 2: "Oh cool, are they having a baptism party or something?"
PERSON 1: "No, they're Muslim. It's just a brunch gathering for a few friends."

‣ *What bias was revealed?*

Next Time You Meet Someone

The next time you have a first encounter with someone, especially if you think you may have biased instincts or assumptions, try to ask yourself some or all of these questions in the moment. They will challenge you to slow down, think critically and avoid letting bias into your first impression.

- Does this person remind you of yourself in any ways? How does this affect your perception of them?

- Do they remind you of anyone else? If so, in a positive or negative way?

- Are there specific things about this person that are influencing your impression?

- Are they things this person has control over or just unchangeable parts of who they are?

- What assessments are you already making about them? Are these assessments based on solid details about their actions and words, or about assumptions you have about them as a person?

Questions for a Bias-Free First Impression

So you have some questions on hand that you can use to track your own assumptions and bias. But what if bias seeps into the questions you ask someone when you're having a first encounter and conversation with them? These could be questions that assume someone's educational background or religion, that subtly try to gather more information about their race or sexuality (when this is information they would only choose to share if comfortable) or that pass some small judgement about their appearance or part of their identity.

The goal of your first time meeting someone should be to learn about who they are as an individual without making any assessments based on their social identities and groups. Their gender, age, sexuality, race, disability (if applicable) and background are things they don't have control over. So basing your impression on any of those things means you're acting on bias. Instead, focus on *who* they are. Asking some of the following questions can help you go deeper with someone you're just getting to know and learn about what makes them unique.

- What hobbies and interests are you passionate about?

- Do you have any favourite places near here where you love to spend time?

- What's the best/most interesting thing that's happened to you this week?

Circle of Trust Exercise

This is a version of an exercise commonly done at anti-bias workshops and trainings, which aims to help you explore and examine the diversity in your closest relationships. Follow the prompts below.

On a piece of paper or in a journal, list the names of the six people you trust most who aren't related to you. Now go through each of these criteria and put a mark next to a person's name in the list for each of the attributes below that they share with you:

- Gender
- Race/ethnicity
- Age (within about ten years)
- Sexual orientation
- Religious beliefs

- Nationality
- Native language
- Educational/ professional background

Reflection

Look at how many marks you have next to the names on your list. Do they indicate that you choose people in your life who are overwhelmingly similar to you, or did you find a solid diversity in your circle of trust? How might this affect your unconscious biases? Might it benefit you to have more variety of perspectives in your close circle?

Journaling Exercise:
Questioning Yourself

As you work through the complex, ongoing process of conquering your unconscious biases, it never hurts to do mental check-ins. You can take a few moments each week or each day to reflect internally on any recent situations where you may have felt or expressed bias and how you can learn from those experiences.

Here are some possible questions to ask yourself:

- Did you make any snap judgements today that felt based on biased instincts rather than evidence? If you slowed down, would you have seen the situation differently?

- Did you find yourself making any comment today about someone else, along the lines of "this only happened because X" or "I don't think I can trust X with Y"? Why do you think you made this assumption?

- Is there a way you could reframe how you thought about that person or situation?

- Did your emotions affect your decision-making this week?

- Were there any times when you felt an urge to make an assumption but managed to catch yourself and reframe it?

Visualization Exercise: Part 1

As you read this passage, try to visualize the details as clearly as possible:

You're heading out to go to a housewarming party at your friend's place. Your friend told you there's someone at the party she wants to set you up with. On the way you stop at the store to grab snacks. The cashier asks where you're heading and you mention the party. Your news app chimes and you read that there was an armed robbery nearby and a suspect was apprehended. You hurry to the party and meet the person your friend is setting you up with. You also talk with a friend of the host, who you find out works nearby as a nurse.

Once you've finished this visualization, consider these questions:

- **What did the cashier at the store look like? How old were they?**

- **Did you picture the robbery suspect? What race were they? What gender?**

- **What did the person your friend introduced you to at the party look like? Did they look like the people you typically date?**

- **What was the gender of the nurse you met? Did you assume anything about their sexuality?**

What do the details of your mental image indicate about your unconscious biases?

Spotting Social Media Bias: Part 1

Social media is one of the strongest sources of bias that we have daily access to. It may be a reinforcer of biases that you already have, perpetuate stereotypes you've been conditioned to believe or put hateful rhetoric in your path.

Avoiding bias on social media is more about learning to see it rather than getting rid of it altogether.

If you use social media (photo-sharing platforms, in particular), try this exercise:

Open up the app you use most often.

Scroll through for five minutes, but rather than doing so mindlessly, be very attentive and focused. Note your observations on paper if possible.

As you go, consider these questions:

- How many of these images are likely to have been altered, edited or filtered to make the subject or model look better?

- How many posts are trying to sell me or convince me of something? How do they use bias to do so?

- Do all the posts feature people who look just like me and share my social groups?

Reflect:

- How might the posts that you're constantly seeing on social media reinforce your own personal unconscious biases?

- Might social media also be perpetuating any negative self-biases and self-images that you have?

- Did you feel like you saw a diversity of perspectives on your social media feeds that will help you learn new things from a variety of people?

Part 2:

- After reflecting on the questions, scroll through for another five minutes.

- This time, go into it with your list of unconscious biases and self-biases (see page 85) in front of you.

- Look for how many posts and ads specifically reinforce or target *these* biases.

- Are ads targeting you based on your gender and the stereotypes associated with it? Are they only showing you images of people who look "picture perfect" with unrealistic bodies and beauty ideals? Are they only showing you people with the same skin colour as you?

- Do the people you choose to follow also encourage any of these stereotypes or biases? Do their captions or comments promote acceptance and awareness or do they show subtle biases (now that you know how to spot these)?

Three Ways to Improve Your Social Media Experience

Social media can be overwhelmingly toxic and packed with false images, bias, misinformation and hate. There are simple ways to start to undo the harmful parts of social media and get a more positive experience from it.

Here are a few tips:

1 **Stop feeling guilty about unfollowing or unfriending.** Seriously. If you have random relatives or acquaintances posting racist, sexist, biased commentary on social media, stop letting that into your brain. When it's hurting you or affecting your unconscious bias, it's not worth having around. You don't have to be friends with everyone. Cut ties when needed.

2 **Purposely follow accounts or people who encourage you.** There are many pages on Instagram and Twitter that focus on things like body positivity, feminism, anti-racism, acceptance and empathy. There are accounts spreading factual, well-researched information on important topics. Seek these out and learn from them instead of biased sources.

3 **Take breaks.** Don't let social media consume you. When you feel the bias creeping in, step back. For as long as you need. It'll still be there when you're ready.

Should You Respond to Bias Online?

Social media is probably one of the most biased places that exists in our world today. Anonymity and a lack of real-world consequences make people online feel invincible. As a collective global platform, it fosters plenty of creativity, connection and positivity, as well as a startling amount of hate. You've likely seen racist comments on Facebook posts, sexist jokes, misleading or false information posted to stir up controversy, content blatantly supporting discrimination.

If you come across something discriminatory on social media, how do you react? Do you keep scrolling, or do you have the urge to do something about it? Getting into comment wars with people can be draining, and little seems to come of it.

But really, it does have an impact. When people continuously make "microaggressive" comments and offensive statements online and no one calls them out on it, the behaviour is reinforced; they feel it's okay and they keep doing it.

Calling someone out on a biased or discriminatory post may be tough (though you can always just report discriminatory language to the social media platform), but over time it has an impact. And it also shows other people that you don't tolerate bias.

Make a Mental Keyword

Everyone learns and practises self-development differently. One tactic that may help you catch yourself if you start to lean into a bias or act on an assumption is giving yourself a keyword.

Essentially, this is a word you select for yourself – perhaps something funny or snappy but definitely easy to remember – that you can yell at yourself internally when you slip up or find yourself falling into a bad unconscious bias habit.

Not only will this jar you out of those negative or presumptive thought patterns, but it may help you keep track of times when you slipped up. This can be useful if you try out the question prompts from earlier and want to recall times during the day or week when you may have acted on bias. Just think back to times when you used your keyword.

If there is someone you trust that knows about your anti-bias journey, you could also share this keyword with them. They can work with you and say the word to you if they notice you make a comment that might be tinged with bias or assumption.

Step Out of Your Comfort Zone

For this exercise, the only goal is to try something that you've never tried before. And it can be something very simple; in fact, the simpler the better.

- Is there a movie, TV show or type of food that you've never tried because you see it as weird or "not for you"?

- Do you "dislike" foreign films because you have watched so many of them and never liked a single one? Or is it because the absence of people who look or sound like you makes you uncomfortable?

- Is that show or movie that features an all-Black or all-female or all-Asian cast actually something you wouldn't enjoy, or do you just assume that because of a bias you have against that group of people?

- Have you tried foods from India, Central America, Ethiopia, Korea, Jamaica and a host of other countries and cultures? Or do you have a bias about some of those places or foods that has made you assume you won't like them?

- This week, choose one of these simple things, try it and see if you can disprove an assumption.

Substitution Exercise

Take a moment to think about the way that your country or area treats a group of people that you don't belong to. This could be white people, Black people, people of another race, immigrants, people with disabilities, LGBTQ+ people, or religious minorities.

Choose one of those groups.

- Now picture living a week in your country as someone who does fit in that group.
- Picture going about the normal parts of life that you already do – work, school, shopping, social gatherings, whatever the case may be.
- Visualize some of the interactions you may have. Picture yourself asking for a raise or promotion. Would you feel more or less confident?
- Picture yourself passing by a police officer. Would you feel more or less comfortable?
- Visualize yourself walking alone at night. Would you feel more or less safe?
- Picture yourself going to a medical appointment. Would you feel more or less confident that you were getting good care and information?

Do you feel more comfortable with your own identity or the one you're picturing? Does this tell you anything about bias in our society, or bias that you feel?

Visualization Exercise: Part 2

Read the following scenario and picture it in as much detail as possible.

You run to catch a flight and greet the flight attendant, who lets you on the plane just before closing the doors. The pilot says hello as you make your way to your seat. The happy couple sitting next to you tells you about the anniversary trip they are heading home from. When you get to your destination, you check in at the hotel and a staff member shows you to your room. You head downstairs to the conference where the CEO of a major company will be speaking. You take a seat and the keynote speaker walks out onto the stage.

Once you've finished the visualization, consider these questions:

- What was the gender of the flight attendant? What did they look like?
- What about the pilot?
- Was the couple next to you heterosexual, or otherwise? How old were they?
- How old was the hotel staff member? What did they look like?
- What did the CEO look like? What was their gender?

What do you think your mental images suggest about unconscious biases you may have?

Exercise: Combatting Hiring Biases

As mentioned before, there are a variety of specific biases associated uniquely with the hiring process. These have been studied and coined by various researchers and psychologists over the course of many decades investigating bias. This exercise is an interesting way to test your bias and learn more, but you can also use this questioning format when you're actually in a hiring situation in your workplace.

For this exercise, picture yourself as a hiring manager.

Now, picture a job applicant in your head (real or imagined). Visualize them in detail – what they look like, their age, gender, sexuality, education, work experience and so on.

Visualize the employee they would be replacing (real or imagined). Run through an imaginary interview in which you (or you and a hiring team) ask several questions of the applicant, after which you need to make a decision about the interview's outcome.

Now answer the following prompts in your head or jot down your notes on a piece of paper. Each of these questions corresponds to a unique form of bias, noted in parentheses.

(Affect heuristics) **Did any superficial aspect of this person's appearance immediately make you disqualify them? Why?**

(Expectation anchor) Do you have any expectations about the person who needs to fill this position? Did that make you judge the applicant differently? Did you project any expectations onto the applicant?

(Halo effect) Did any aspect of this person's background or experience make you favour them too highly?

(Similarity attraction bias) Is the person you're visualizing similar to you in any ways? Does this influence your perception of them?

(Horn effect) Was there anything about the candidate that was off-putting to you and made you want to stop considering them? Why did this one thing overshadow their good qualities?

(Beauty bias) Was the person you visualized attractive or unattractive? Did this affect your opinion of them?

(Conformity bias) Was your opinion of this person influenced by what you thought others might think of your decision?

Reflect on all of these reactions. Then, if you're feeling compelled to, try the exercise again and picture someone entirely different from the first candidate. See how your answers change.

Visualizing People Exercise

Like the previous visualization exercises, this one will offer up simple scenarios of people engaged in a situation. Picture each one quickly and instinctually and see what comes to mind first.

Visualize someone outside a store yelling and being handcuffed by police.
What does this person look like? Why do you picture them this way?

Visualize someone dancing in a bar surrounded by friends and wearing a colourful, festive outfit.
What does this person look like? Why do you picture them this way?

Visualize someone standing at the head of a boardroom, speaking to a group of employees.
What does this person look like? Why do you picture them this way?

Visualize someone volunteering at a homeless shelter on the weekend.
What does this person look like? Why do you picture them this way?

After visualizing, assess whether any of your mental images were based on unconscious biases. In future attempts, try picturing the opposite of your natural assumption, to fight unconscious biases.

Exercise: Tracking Sources of Bias

Try this exercise over the course of a week to get a better idea of where bias comes from in your life.

All week, pay extra attention to any sources pushing biased ideals on you. Photoshopped images, hateful social media posts and comments, backhanded remarks from family members or friends, biased advertising, favouritism and stereotyping in your workplace, and so on. Try to notice as much as possible. Each time you see bias coming into contact with you from an outside source, make a short note or tally of the bias and where it came from. Add details when helpful. At the end of the week, see where most of your external bias comes from. How can you try to limit the effect this has on you?

Building Empathy Through Three Exercises

Empathy is bias's worst nightmare. If you're understanding and sharing someone else's feelings, you are accepting them and connecting to them, even if you don't know them personally. That leaves no room for bias.

Building up your range of empathetic abilities is a great technique to help you progress in your anti-biased journey.

Exercise 1: Reverse engineering

For this exercise, visualize someone you'd like to understand better. Perhaps a boss or relative or romantic interest who you can never get a good read on. Then picture the last interaction you had with them that was particularly confusing to you, one that left you completely unsure what they were thinking or feeling.

Now, as closely as you can, recreate, imitate and embody how they acted, looked and sounded in that encounter. Think about their facial expressions, body language, tone, words and so on. Repeat it, picturing yourself in their place.

What do you find when you re-enact the situation as them? You may find yourself experiencing an emotion you don't expect, the one they may have been feeling without you realizing it at the time.

Exercise 2: Empathetic eavesdropping

When you're sitting in a cafe or park, relaxing, do you ever find yourself unconsciously listening in on the conversations around you? You may not eagerly or intentionally eavesdrop, but do you naturally start to pick up on what others are talking about?

Try (politely) doing this on purpose. As you sit in a public space, listen to a brief conversation. Here's the key thing: do so with *no judgement whatsoever*. Instead, use this as an opportunity to practise empathy. Without knowing anything about this person or people, listen to a bit of what they're saying and try to feel their emotions. Learn something about them through empathy, rather than superficial judgements and bias.

Exercise 3: Kindness meditation

Breathe calmly. With every breath out, send positive thoughts and love to yourself. After five minutes, start sending these kind thoughts to someone you care about. After a few more minutes, adjust your energy and channel the kind thoughts to someone you don't like, or to a stranger you might have bias toward.

If you can send kindness to yourself and to a loved one, you should also be able to build the skills over time to send it to others.

Exercise: Active Listening

Another exercise for building empathy is learning to listen actively. Do you ever find yourself in a conversation listening to someone else but truly just waiting until it's your "turn" to talk? If that's the case, you're not actually listening, and you're certainly not *actively listening*.

When you listen actively, you're completely engaged with what the other person is saying. You pick up on things like their body language and tone, you understand their feelings and you get a more complete picture of who they are. This helps you get to know someone without bias.

Try this exercise with someone you already know well, then with someone you would like to get to know better.

- First, ask someone how they're doing.

- If they respond with "fine" or "alright", don't just accept this and move on.

- Follow up with, "Are you sure? How are you *really* doing?"

- Make eye contact, use warm body language, make it clear that you're engaged in whatever they have to say.

- See if they open up more. If they do, continue active listening using some of the techniques on the next page.

Conversation Dos and Don'ts

A bias-free, non-judgmental, productive conversation should always be your goal, whether you're talking to someone you've known for a long time or talking to someone for the first time. There are plenty of things to avoid if you want to keep up this good conversational mojo, and plenty of things to do instead.

Here are some places to start.

In conversations, don't:

- Interrupt.

- Get distracted.

- Obsess over tiny details and miss the point of what they're saying.

- "One up" the story with one of your own.

- Let bias influence how you react.

- Use offensive language.

- Bring up things you know will hurt or bother someone.

- Rush the other person.

To have great conversations:

- Make eye contact.

- Have open, engaged body language.

- Use a positive, productive tone.

- Be sensitive of the triggers and feelings of the person you're talking to, whenever possible.

- Listen to the full story.

- Get to the bottom of things, listen for the deeper meaning.

- Use accepting, empathetic words and phrases.

Noticing and Tackling "Positive" Stereotypes

Benevolent bias. Positive stereotypes. They mean the same thing. They're still bias and still stereotypes, and they still hurt people, they just look and sound nicer on the surface.

Saying women are good at homemaking is bias. Always asking your male friend to help you build furniture because he's a man is stereotyping. So is asking your classmate to help you with something on the computer because they're Asian. You may be assuming that they're good at something (thus seeing it as a compliment), but you're assuming that because of a stereotype about their race or social group.

So, next time you ask someone to help you with something or do an activity with you, ask yourself these questions first:

- Why am I asking this particular person?

- Is it because I know they have an expertise or love of a subject, or because I assume they do?

- Have I witnessed this person enjoying or doing this thing before?

- Is there someone else I know who may be more able to help me or enjoy this more?

Exercise: Questioning Familial Bias

Our families are often the first exposure we have to bias and prejudice from a young age. This changes quickly as we go to school and are influenced by other children (who are influenced by their own families) and teachers, go online, and later as we gain more independence, get jobs, make friends and so on.

Your family's biases may have been crystal-clear to you and remain obvious now. Or they may be harder to see. Regardless, recognizing the biases you learned as a child can help you spot some that you may still cling to as an adult. Here are some questions you can ask yourself to uncover some of the more unconscious biases your family may have instilled:

- As a child, did my family present particular people, groups or situations as "normal"? Did they present other people or groups as "weird"?

- What kinds of TV programmes and movies was I allowed to watch as a kid? Did this give me a diverse perspective of the world or a biased one?

- When my parents heard offensive or prejudiced comments, did they discuss them and shut them down, or laugh and encourage them?

- Were there people that my parents or family told me to avoid?

Exercise: Uncovering Bias on the News

If you watch, read or listen to the news, you are consuming biased information at some time or another. Even the most "bias-free" stations and websites still have to employ a wide range of reporters, writers and editors. And since all of us have some unconscious biases, somewhere among that mix, bias will be added in, whether unintentionally or purposefully. Some news sources don't hide their bias. They openly support particular political opinions and take active stances. These can inform you but not about all sides of an issue. When you consume news in some form, it is likely to influence your unconscious biases, which is why it's important to be more critical about your news gathering as you work to undo your biases.

If you're watching or reading a piece of news, these are some questions you can ask to uncover bias:

- **Is this a reported news story or an opinion piece?**
  (Start here; if it's intended to be opinion, then exposing bias is less of an issue.)

- **What words are being used?**
  (Quality-assigning adjectives like *great*, *bad*, *awful*, *excellent* and so on indicate an opinion being given. Assess whether the opinion indicates an unnecessary or inappropriate bias.)

- Is favouritism being shown to anyone involved here? Is someone being presumed guilty before trial? Is one politician's opinion getting more screen time or being presented with more favourable wording?
  (This takes a little more comparison to note but is a great indictor of bias.)

- Does the source avoid certain relevant topics altogether, because they may contradict a point they want to make?
  (If there's a part of the story or something related clearly missing, it may be because it would discredit their stance.)

- Are there sources cited? Are those sources credible, relevant and unbiased?
  (If there is reporting being done, relying on expert sources is crucial, so a lack of good cited and credible sources indicates that something may be amiss with the source.)

- Is the main argument or point proven with solid evidence?
  (If the main point of the article or news segment doesn't have a solid evidentiary basis, the reporting is sloppy and may not be reliable.)

- Who is the reporter or writer? What backgrounds do they come from? How might this affect their bias?

Exercise: Choosing Your Sources

If you're writing an article, working on an academic paper or doing a research study, or even just trying to learn more about any topic, how do you choose the sources you'll rely on and refer to? Do you click on the first link that a basic search pulls up or do you dig a little deeper to find credible, less biased sources?

As you seek out sources, for whatever reason, consider these questions to help you determine if you're using a source that's helping you rather than hurting you:

- What are the author's credentials? Is the author an expert on this topic?

- What is the publication/site's reliability?

- How old is the material? How important is timeliness for this topic?

- What is the author's background? Do they have any potential reason to be biased? Do they bring a diverse or appropriate perspective?

- Do they use opinionated language? If so, is this appropriate in the context?

- Was the information reviewed by others before publishing?

Reflection Exercise: Media You Consume

The content and information you take in does a lot to influence you – it may make you more informed about more diverse topics and perspectives or it may keep you closed in a box of similar stories and narratives.

This exercise asks you to consider some of the most recent sources of information and media you have consumed and then to reflect on the effect those choices may have on your self-empowerment.

Exercise questions:

- What are the last three books you read?
- What are the last three articles you read/podcasts you listened to?
- What are the three websites or platforms you go to most often for news?

Reflection questions:

- Look into the authors of those books and articles, and the casts and creators of those movies and podcasts. Are you consuming media from a diverse range of perspectives?
- Are the news platforms you use known for particular biases or slants? Do you keep this in mind when reading their content?

Take time to reflect on all of your answers and what they've shown you about the diversity or bias in the media you consume.

Questions to Uncover Workplace Bias

As discussed in the previous chapter, the workplace is one of the places where unconscious bias is revealed most often. Between hiring discrimination, sexual harassment, bullying, derogatory language, pay gaps, preferential treatment and unfairness in raises and promotions, there can be many issues at play.

If you do think your workplace has some real issues with bias, whether among management or employees, these are also good questions to ask yourself or to discuss with your co-workers before bringing a report forward.

- Have you ever experienced any type of harassment (these can be small or large things, like frequent "harmless" teasing, touching, inappropriate language, hazing and so on) by another employee or a boss?

- Have you ever heard a derogatory comment in the workplace that was tolerated by people around you?

- Have you ever had someone at work make an assumption about you as a person or your work performance that felt unfounded or irrational?

- Have you ever felt you or a colleague received treatment that differed from someone else's for no clear reason?

- Does your workplace have a dress code or other policies that favour some groups over others?

Exercise: Investigating Bias in Your Workplace

If the previous questions raised some red flags about your workplace, this exercise is a good continuation to help you explore some other possible forms of bias that could exist at work.

For this visualization exercise, picture your current workplace, or the one you worked at most recently.

Now picture the last three people that were hired by your company (or if it's too large a company, in your department).

Next, picture the last three people that resigned from your company from your company or department.

Finally, picture the last three people who were promoted or given a raise in your company or department.

Reflection

- Do the people you picture in each category have anything in common? Do you see any patterns in the types of people your company hires, fires or promotes?

- Are there any types of people notably missing from any of these categories?

- What might this indicate about the bias in the management at your company?

The Power of Words

There are a lot of words in any language that cause harm. They hurt people or communities. They show our bias or prejudice. They're derogatory and offensive. Some of these words are considered too offensive to be said at all. Other words are still commonplace, but hurtful, to whatever degree.

This exercise asks you to think about any words that you personally use that might hurt someone or be biased or offensive. This includes racist, sexist, homophobic, ableist language, but also any words that are old-fashioned, outdated or that you know you use in a way that could offend someone.

On a piece of paper, underneath the heading "Biased Words to Avoid", list these words. Write down anything that you ever think or say that you wish you didn't or realize you shouldn't. Be honest and don't judge yourself; you're growing.

Then, in a column to the right with the heading "Empathetic Words to Activate", list positive words. These should be words that could replace the ones on the left; more unbiased choices, more thoughtful phrases, more empathetic ways of talking about people, words you love and wish you used more.

Unbiased in the Real World: How to Be an Ally

Allyship is a concept that's emerged in recent years in light of movements for racial justice and social equality for various groups facing discrimination. In essence, being an ally is being outside of a group but finding any possible way to support the justice of those who are facing prejudice, bias and discrimination.

Allyship goes beyond not being biased or not discriminating. It means taking a more active role in your world. Here are some simple ways you can show that you genuinely support the people around you who come from different backgrounds or are facing discrimination.

- Start by fostering an atmosphere of openness. This could apply to your home, your workplace or anywhere you're interacting with people. Make it clear to the people in your life that you are open and ready to talk about biases, discrimination or any other things weighing on them.

- Then aim for the opposite of microaggressions: microaffirmations. Simple and subtle kindnesses go a long way. Give your attention to marginalized people. Make it clear that you value their time. Offer genuine praise and compliments and use open, encouraging body language. Stay engaged.

How to Support Friends Sensitively

If you're close with someone of another race or from another social group, it's natural to want to be there for them when something is happening in the world that would impact their mental health (for example, widespread racial violence and protests). But there are good ways and bad ways to check in. Follow these tips to reach out more thoughtfully.

- Just listen. Be a good friend. If they want to vent or release some emotions, let them. Be there to provide a kind and engaged ear.

- Never make it about you. This is not your experience. Even if you've experienced other discrimination, this is their own experience. If they're talking about the racial discrimination they're experiencing, it is not the time to mention something else you've been through.

- Don't virtue signal. Basically this means that even if you're taking steps to be a great ally – you went to protests or donated to helpful organizations – your friend doesn't need the list of why you're a good person. Do it without needing the praise, just because it's the right thing to do.

" When someone else's safety and acceptance in society is on the line, your personal discomfort comes in a very distant second.

COURTNEY MILAN

Reacting to Bias in Your Interactions

While much of the focus of this book and this chapter is on your internal process to discover unconscious biases and learn ways to reframe or eliminate them, it is also hard to witness other people speaking or acting with bias and discrimination and not do anything about it. This is a huge step in being an ally.

If you are out in your daily life and hear someone make a sexist, racist, homophobic, ableist, xenophobic or otherwise discriminatory remark, or see them treat someone in a biased or hateful way, it likely will (and should) affect you.

The hard part and the next step is doing something about it. Many of us struggle with this. We've heard something that bothers us, either because it was discriminatory towards ourselves or because it was offensive to another group and we want to stand up for members of our community. But we fear confrontation or lack confidence to go up to someone and tell them that they're being biased or offensive. This is normal, but we have to fight the fear.

Here are a few tips to speak up and be heard in a safe and productive way:

- Practise and build confidence before confrontation. Visualize scenarios of real-world discrimination that you've witnessed in the past and things you wish you'd said. Practise aloud some assertive responses you could use the next time you hear a racist comment or derogatory language.

- Choose confrontation only when it's safe. If it's late and there are no bystanders present, it's probably best to let it slide. Don't put your safety at risk over one comment. If you see other people around who can stand up for you, the situation is safer for confrontation.

- Be assertive, not aggressive. Coming into an interaction yelling and being verbally abusive isn't productive. Approach them and calmly but firmly explain what you felt was discriminatory about their words/actions and why.

- Don't make it about you if it's not. If someone is making racist comments toward another person, be a good ally and support them. But don't speak for their feelings and say "you offended this person". Speak for yourself. "Your language is derogatory and not okay," for example.

Exercise: A Full Unbiased Day

By now you have many exercises, prompts and techniques to use in your actively unbiased self-empowerment work. For one final cumulative exercise, once you've mastered some of the other exercises, spend one day doing as many as you can.

This will be the ultimate challenge. It's not easy thinking critically and continuously acting on empathy rather than bias. But you can do it.

Try to do several of the following in the same day. At the end, reflect on what the experience taught you. Do you feel drained, uplifted, frustrated, rewarded? No matter your feeling, remind yourself that this journey is worth the effort. Carry on.

1 Talk to an acquaintance or stranger and practise active listening. Follow up by questioning yourself with the prompts on page 116.

2 Do the social media exercise from pages 102–103. Or take a social media break and see how it affects you.

3 Try reverse engineering, from page 114.

4 Question the news you consume.

5 Answer the reflection questions from page 125 while in your workplace.

6 Do a kindness meditation as shown on page 115.

Record Your Day

Final Reflection Questions

You have nearly reached the end of this book and a
large journey of exercises and prompts to help you
explore and defeat your unconscious biases. So it
seems fitting to include some final questions that
provide an extra opportunity to reflect on the things
you've learned throughout this process of uncoupling
from your bias.

These are questions you can consider at any point in
the process. You can return to them more than once.
You can come back to them every few months or every
year to see if things have changed. If you want to take
any notes, write them in a journal and keep it handy.

Remember that this is an ongoing, lifelong process.
As long as there is bias in the world, there will be reason
to work against it, in your own mind and actions, and
out in your community. If you want to take any notes,
write them on the following pages, or in a journal.

Internal reflection questions

- What have I learned about myself in this process
  that I didn't know before I started?

- At what points have I been tempted to judge
  myself?

- Have I improved my self-love throughout this
  process? Have I defeated any self-biases?

- Has my perspective of the world shifted in any
  specific ways?

- How often do I find myself questioning my unconscious biases?

- Do I act or speak with bias less often?

- Have I slowed down in my speaking and decision-making to be more thoughtful?

- Have I developed any new empathy skills?

External reflection questions

- Have I learned new ways to evaluate social media?

- Am I a more critical media consumer?

- Have I developed any more diversity in my social connections, workplace, sources, media and interactions?

- Have I had any good first impressions and first encounters that might have previously gone poorly?

- Have I taken any new steps to combat bias in the workplace?

- Have I made any steps to respond to bias on social media or with my family?

- Have I made any productive steps to being a good real-world ally?

Final Reflections

Final Thoughts

This book set out with one true goal: to introduce you to bias in its many forms and to train you to conquer it. If you feel more aware and attuned to bias and how it works, this book has met its goal. If you feel like you've taken any steps to become more unbiased, all the better.

Remember: there is no such thing as a one-time fix. Being unbiased is a lifelong process, something you keep working at, a little every day. Some days will be harder than others.

There is so much to be said for the fact that you made it this far. You did the reading, you opened yourself up to learning about bias and maybe some truths about yourself that weren't easy to accept. The truth of any self-empowerment journey is that some parts won't be fun, but the result will be a better you and a process that was worth whatever you put into it. So put in as much effort and commitment as you can.

Take what you learned here and bring it into your life. Shut down those little biased thoughts and open yourself up to meeting people without judgements. Let go of the biases you have about yourself, just as much as the ones you have about strangers. Question everything the world tries to tell you is true; decide for yourself. Think critically and listen actively. Go out and be the ally that so many groups of people need. You will be grateful to have them as allies when you need them yourself.

And remember this book will always be here. You can return to it whenever you need to; the exercises and questions in these pages are designed to be used again and again, whenever they serve a purpose in your life. Share them with your friends, family or colleagues. Or simply share what you've learned. This work does not have to be entirely solitary; in fact, it really shouldn't be.

Remember, the more of us who learn to leave our biases behind, the more acceptance and love we add to the world.

Further reading

Books:

Between the World and Me by Ta-Nehisi Coates (2015)

Biased: Uncovering the Hidden Prejudice that Shapes What We See, Think, and Do by Jennifer Eberhardt, PhD (2020)

Blind Spot: Hidden Biases of Good People by Mahzarin R. Banaji and Anthony G. Greenwald (2016)

Body Positive Power: How to Stop Dieting, Make Peace with Your Body and Live by Megan Jayne Crabbe (2017)

Disability Visibility: First Person Stories from the Twenty-First Century by Alice Wong (2020)

Empathy: Why It Matters, and How to Get It by Roman Krznaric (2015)

Haben: The Deafblind Woman Who Conquered Harvard Law by Haben Girma (2019)

How to Be an Antiracist by Ibram X. Kendi (2019)

In a Day's Work: The Fight to End Sexual Violence Against America's Most Vulnerable Workers by Bernice Yeung (2018)

Know My Name: The Survivor of the Stanford Sexual Assault Case Tells Her Story by Chanel Miller (2019)

Shrill: Notes From a Loud Woman by Lindy West (2017)

Tell Me How It Ends: An Essay in Forty Questions by Valeria Luiselli (2017)

Transgender History: The Roots of Today's Revolution by Susan Stryker (2017)

We Are Everywhere: Protest, Power, and Pride in the History of Queer Liberation by Matthew Riemer and Leighton Brown (2019)

Why I'm No Longer Talking to White People About Race by Reni Eddo-Lodge (2018)

Websites:

AllSides: www.allsides.com

American Press Institute : www.americanpressinstitute.org

Amnesty International: www.amnesty.org.uk

Catalyst: catalyst.org

Look Different: www.lookdifferent.org

Project Implicit (online bias tests, as well as resources): implicit.harvard.edu

World Health Organization: www.who.int

Reliable News Sources:

Associated Press

BBC

The Bureau of Investigative Journalism

Pew Research Center

Reuters

The New York Times

The Wall Street Journal

Sources and Articles for Further Reading:

These articles were accessed and consulted for research purposes in 2020 and new research is being done on these topics all the time. While these are all great sources of information, always check out the timeliness of your reading. There are great studies and articles from years past, and there will also be great new things coming in the future to help you stay up to date on these topics.

"6 Ways to Overcome Your Biases for Good" by Alice Boyes, PhD

https://www.psychologytoday.com/us/blog/in-practice/201508/6-ways-overcome-your-biases-good

"How to become a less biased version of yourself" by Tomas Chamorro-Premuzic

https://www.fastcompany.com/90303107/how-to-become-a-less-biased-version-of-yourself

"Test Yourself for Hidden Bias"

https://www.tolerance.org/professional-development/test-yourself-for-hidden-bias

"The Empathy Workout" by Martha Beck